KOFI KINGSTON

BY MATT SCHEFF

PRO WRESTLING SUPERSTARS

Published by ABDO Publishing Company, PO Box 398166, Minneapolis, MN 55439. Copyright © 2014 by Abdo Consulting Group, Inc. International copyrights reserved in all countries. No part of this book may be reproduced in any form without written permission from the publisher. SportsZone™ is a trademark and logo of ABDO Publishing Company.

Printed in the United States of America,
North Mankato, Minnesota
082013
012014

♻ THIS BOOK CONTAINS AT LEAST 10% RECYCLED MATERIALS.

Editor: Chrös McDougall
Series Designer: Jake Nordby

Photo Credits: Mike Lano Photojournalism, cover, cover (background), 1, 1 (background), 24-25, 30 (top); Moses Robinson/Getty Images, 4-5; Matt May/AP Images for Sears Holdings Corp., 6-7; Carrie Devorah/WENN.com/Newscom, 8 (inset); Matt Roberts/Zuma Press/Icon SMI, 8 (inset), 16-17, 20-21; Revelli-Beaumont/ SIPA/Newscom, 10-11, 14-15; Jim R. Bounds/AP Images for WWE, 12-13; Sebastian Kahnert/dpa/picture-alliance/Newscom, 18-19; Jim R. Bounds/AP Images for WWE, 19 (inset); Panoramic/Imago/Icon SMI, 22; Daniel Reyes/Newscom, 23; Panoramic/ Imago/Icon SMI, 26-27, 26 (inset) 30 (bottom), 31; Zuma Press/Icon SMI, 28-29

Library of Congress Control Number: 2013945681

Cataloging-in-Publication Data

Scheff, Matt.
 Kofi Kingston / Matt Scheff.
   p. cm. -- (Pro wrestling superstars)
Includes index.
ISBN 978-1-62403-136-6
1. Kingston, Kofi, 1981- --Juvenile literature. 2. Wrestlers--United States--Biography-- Juvenile literature. 3. Wrestlers--Ghana--Biography--Juvenile literature.1. Title.
796.812092--dc23
[B]

                                                                2013945681

CONTENTS

FIRST-TIME CHAMP

Kofi Kingston was in trouble. He was wrestling for World Wrestling Entertainment's (WWE's) intercontinental championship. But Chris Jericho seemed to be in control of the match. Jericho had Kingston in a powerful hold and was about to go for the pin. But then WWE legend Shawn Michaels charged out to the ring. He distracted Jericho while Kingston got to his feet.

Now Kingston was ready. Jericho turned around. As soon as he did, Kingston charged, leaped into the air, and kicked Jericho in the head. *One, two, three!* It was over. Kingston was the champ!

FAST FACT

The intercontinental title was the first wrestling belt Kingston won.

Kofi Kingston is one of WWE's biggest stars.

MEET KOFI

Kofi Nahaje Sarkodie-Mensah was born August 14, 1981, in Ghana. That country is in western Africa. When Kofi was one, his family moved to Winchester, Massachusetts. Kofi was a gifted athlete. He played basketball. He also was a star wrestler for his high school team. In 1998, he didn't lose a single match all season.

Kofi shows fans his intercontinental belt.

Fast Fact

Kofi never missed a match or a practice in four years of high school wrestling.

After high school,
Kofi went to Boston
College. He studied
communications. Kofi
graduated and started
working at an office job.
But he wasn't happy
there. He remembered
his days as a high school
wrestler. He dreamed of
a career in the ring.

Shawn Michaels was one of WWE's biggest stars during the 1990s and early 2000s.

Kofi dreamed of becoming a professional wrestler.

Kofi has long been a high-flying wrestler.

Kofi followed his dream. He began training as a wrestler. In 2006, he wrestled in his first professional match in a small league called Chaotic Wrestling. His high-flying style was a hit with fans. Kofi went to a WWE tryout at a wrestling school. The WWE officials were impressed. They signed Kofi to a developmental contract in September 2006.

WWE sent Kofi to a small organization called Deep South Wrestling to work on his skills. He wrestled under the name Kofi Nahaje Kingston, but soon dropped the middle name. He said he was from the island of Jamaica. He even spoke with a Jamaican accent.

Primo hits Kofi with a backbreaker during a 2011 match.

13

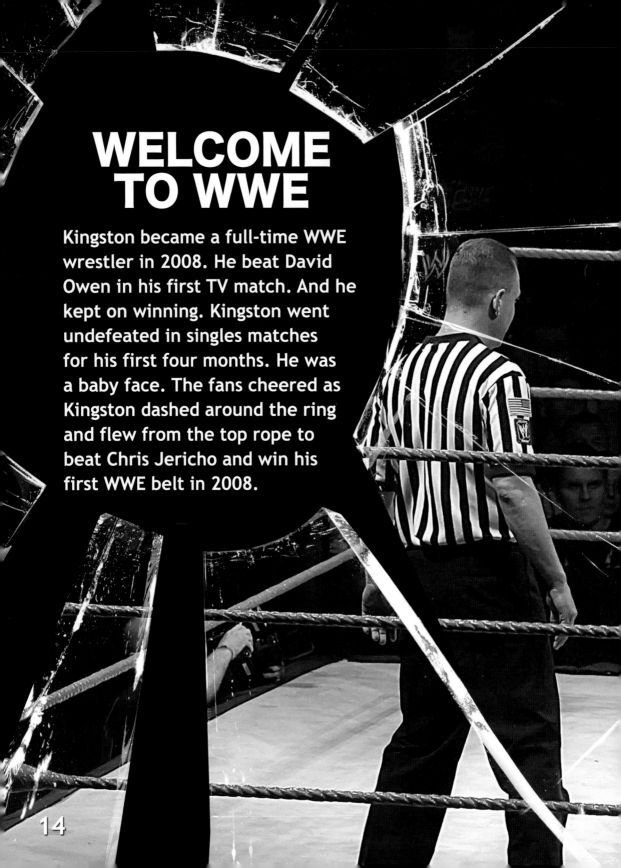

WELCOME TO WWE

Kingston became a full-time WWE wrestler in 2008. He beat David Owen in his first TV match. And he kept on winning. Kingston went undefeated in singles matches for his first four months. He was a baby face. The fans cheered as Kingston dashed around the ring and flew from the top rope to beat Chris Jericho and win his first WWE belt in 2008.

Kingston launches an aerial attack against Santino Marella in 2008.

FAST FACT

Kingston's mother begged him to stop pretending he was from Jamaica. She wanted him to be proud of being from Ghana.

Kingston performs a flying leg drop at WrestleMania 25.

FAST FACT

Kingston is also a master of the Boom Drop. It is a jumping double leg drop. He sometimes jumps from the top rope or ladders and lands on his opponent's head!

Kingston needed his own finishing move. Every WWE star has one. So he created the Trouble in Paradise. In this move, Kingston charges toward his opponent. Then he leaps into the air and spins his body. As he spins, he kicks his opponent hard in the head. It's a difficult move, but it's perfect for Kingston's high-energy style.

THE DREADLOCKED DYNAMO

Kingston kept improving. He formed a tag team with CM Punk. They won the world tag-team title in October 2008. Next, Kingston earned the US championship by beating Montel Vontavious Porter in 2009. Kingston beat Drew McIntyre to win it again the following year. Around this time, Kingston also dropped his Jamaican accent.

Kingston teamed up with CM Punk to win the tag-team title.

FAST FACT

Kingston's hairstyle earned him the nickname "The Dreadlocked Dynamo."

Kingston quickly became a WWE star.

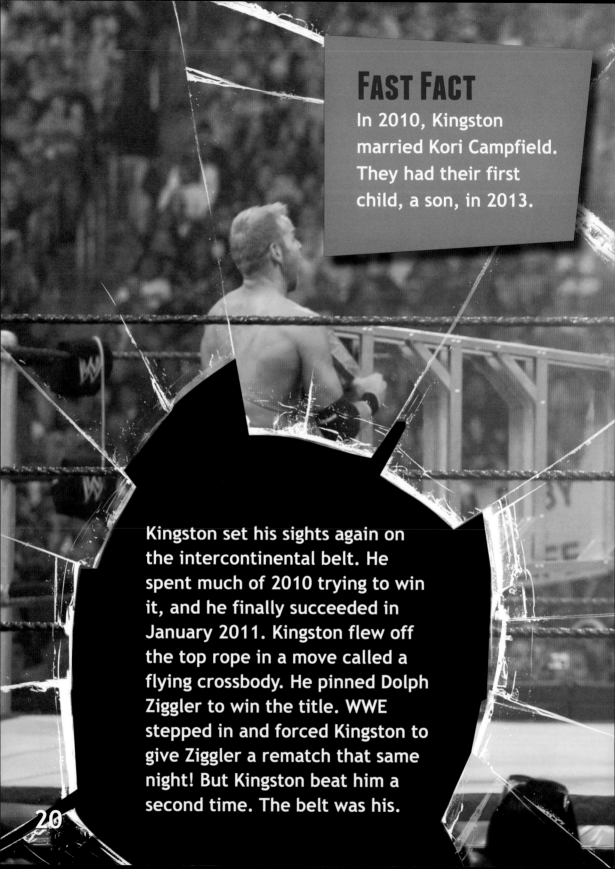

FAST FACT

In 2010, Kingston married Kori Campfield. They had their first child, a son, in 2013.

Kingston set his sights again on the intercontinental belt. He spent much of 2010 trying to win it, and he finally succeeded in January 2011. Kingston flew off the top rope in a move called a flying crossbody. He pinned Dolph Ziggler to win the title. WWE stepped in and forced Kingston to give Ziggler a rematch that same night! But Kingston beat him a second time. The belt was his.

Kingston leaps over a ladder to avoid attack at WrestleMania 25.

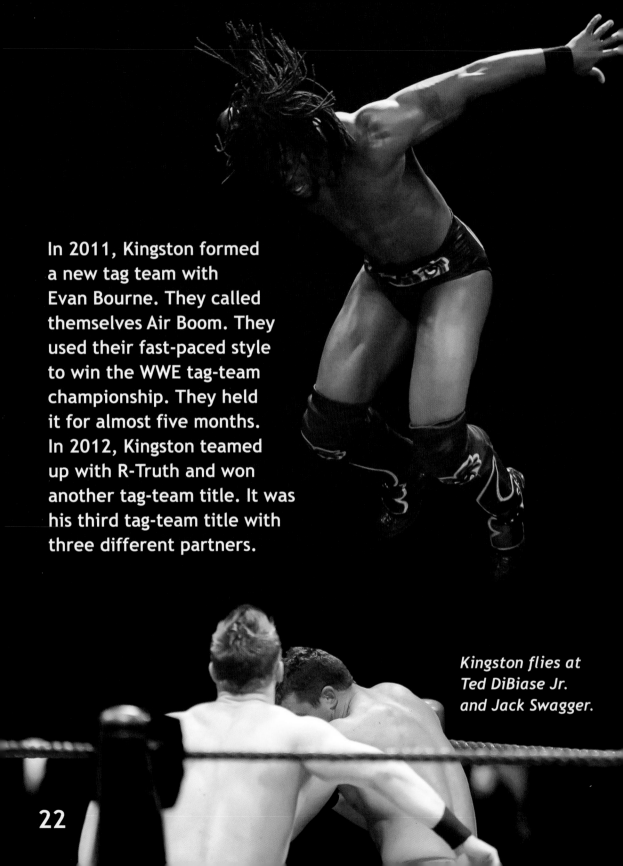

In 2011, Kingston formed a new tag team with Evan Bourne. They called themselves Air Boom. They used their fast-paced style to win the WWE tag-team championship. They held it for almost five months. In 2012, Kingston teamed up with R-Truth and won another tag-team title. It was his third tag-team title with three different partners.

Kingston flies at Ted DiBiase Jr. and Jack Swagger.

Few can handle Kingston's high-flying attacks.

Fast Fact

Pro Wrestling Illustrated named Kingston and R-Truth the tag team of the year in 2012.

Kingston goes for the pin.

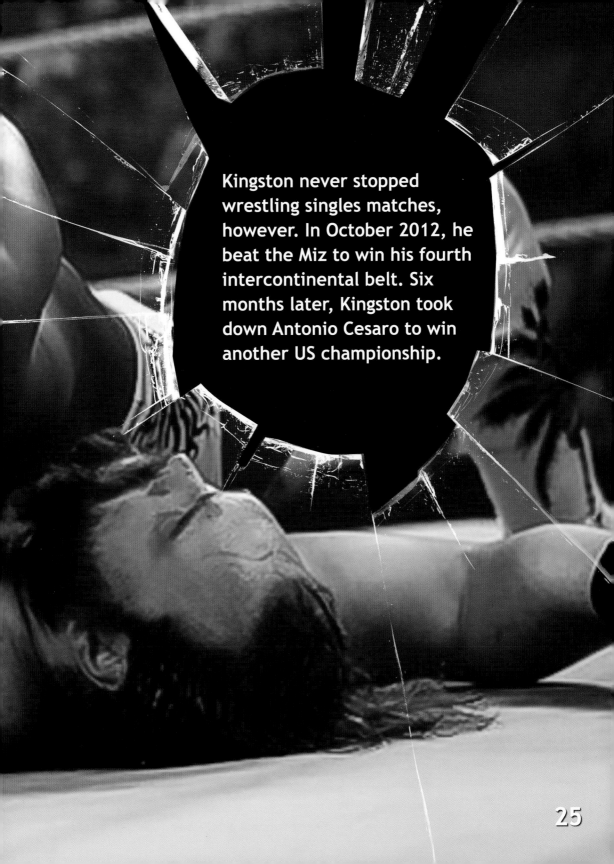

Kingston never stopped wrestling singles matches, however. In October 2012, he beat the Miz to win his fourth intercontinental belt. Six months later, Kingston took down Antonio Cesaro to win another US championship.

THE FUTURE

In May 2013, Ryback defeated Kingston in a match. Ryback continued to attack Kingston after the match was over. He slammed Kingston headfirst into a table. Kingston's neck and elbow were injured. He wasn't able to wrestle again for weeks.

Kingston goes for the pin.

Kofi takes a shot at Matt Hardy.

Kingston has accomplished a lot in his short WWE career. Many WWE wrestlers rely on their raw strength. But Kingston's style is all about big, high-flying moves. His many fans hope that one day he'll be able to beat the best of the best to truly stand atop the professional wrestling world.

Fans hope to watch Kingston's high-flying moves for years to come.

TIMELINE

1981
Kofi Nahaje Sarkodie-Mensah is born August 14, 1981, in Ghana.

1998
Kofi goes undefeated on his high school wrestling team.

2006
Kofi begins his wrestling career and takes the name Kofi Nahaje Kingston.

2008
Kingston joins WWE full time and beats Chris Jericho to win his first WWE belt.

2010
Kingston marries Kori Campfield.

2011
Kingston beats Dolph Ziggler twice in one night to win, then defend, the intercontinental title.

2012
The team of Kingston and R-Truth is named tag team of the year by *Pro Wrestling Illustrated*.

2013
Kingston suffers injuries to his elbow and neck that force him to take a break from wrestling.

GLOSSARY

accent
A way of pronouncing words in a particular language, usually among people of a particular region.

baby face
A wrestler whom fans view as a good guy.

developmental contract
An agreement in which a wrestler signs with WWE but wrestles in smaller leagues to gain experience and develop skills.

finishing move
A powerful move that a wrestler uses to finish off an opponent.

Trouble in Paradise
Kingston's finishing move in which he charges at his standing opponent, leaps, spins, and kicks the opponent in the head.

INDEX